Saving an

AMERICAN SYMBOL

By
Rena Korb

PEARSON

Scott
Foresman

Editorial Offices: Glenview, Illinois • Parsippany, New Jersey • New York, New York
Sales Offices: Needham, Massachusetts • Duluth, Georgia • Glenview, Illinois
Coppell, Texas • Ontario, California • Mesa, Arizona

ISBN: 0-328-13580-1

8 9 10 V0G1 14 13 12 11 10 09 08

Endless Herds

Imagine yourself standing on the Great Plains a couple of hundred years ago. It's springtime. The prairie is bright green with new grass. Suddenly you hear a far off rumble. The sky is cloudless. It can't be thunder. The rumbling grows louder. Then you feel the ground shaking beneath your feet. And finally you see the source. A sea of big brown beasts spills over the horizon. It's a huge herd of American buffalo! Soon thousands of buffalo cover the prairie. They stretch as far as you can see in every direction.

American buffalo on the prairie

Great herds of American buffalo once covered much of the continent. They lived west of the Rocky Mountains, north almost to the **tundra,** throughout the Great Plains, and east of the Mississippi River. Until the mid-1830s, travelers on the Great Plains saw huge buffalo herds almost everywhere. One man reported that he waited five days for a herd to pass. While the animals ran by, he tried to count them. He estimated four million in the herd! When the buffalo finally stopped coming, he measured their trail. It was 18 miles wide! No one imagined that buffalo could ever die out.

BUFFALO or BISON ?

American buffalo are not closely related to the other buffalo of the world. India's water buffalo and Africa's Cape buffalo are true buffaloes. American buffalo have a much bigger head and huge humped shoulders. American buffalo look more like European bison, their closest relatives.

"The Buffalo Hunt" by Paul Kane, 19th century.

Sacred Symbol of Survival

Native Americans hunted buffalo for thousands of years before Europeans came to North America. They hunted the large hoofed animals with bows and arrows or spears. Buffalo were like a supermarket for Plains Indians. They ate buffalo meat and made clothing and shelters from buffalo hides. They used buffalo bones to make tools and weapons. Buffalo hooves were even boiled down to make glue. No part of the buffalo was wasted. Many Native American ceremonies honored the sacred buffalo, from the large bulls to the **scrawny** newborn calves. The tribes depended on them for survival.

Plains Indians depended on buffalo meat and hides for survival. This made the buffalo a sacred animal.

American Buffalo Hunters

Life on the Great Plains changed when the Europeans arrived. The new settlers didn't see the buffalo as a sacred animal to be respected and honored. The Europeans saw buffalo hunting as a way to make money, or something to do for sport. By the early 1800s, American buffalo hunters armed with rifles arrived on the Plains. Soon they were killing thousands and thousands of buffalo.

William F. Cody earned the nickname Buffalo Bill after he killed 4,000 buffalo in just one year.

A Coast-to-Coast Railroad

In the 1860s, construction began on the transcontinental railroad. It would stretch from the Atlantic Ocean to the Pacific. Buffalo hunters followed the growing railroad. Some became famous. Have you ever heard of Buffalo Bill? The buffalo hunters killed the animals to feed the work crews. They also hunted buffalo to keep them off the tracks.

Hunters keep the buffalo off the tracks by shooting them.

Once the transcontinental railroad was finished, things only got worse for the buffalo. Railroad passengers killed buffalo simply for sport. Buffalo **carcasses** soon dotted the Plains. The great dead beasts rotted in the sun. The stench of **decay** was in the air. In 1869 one magazine writer described seeing a railroad train with the passengers "shooting, from every available window, with rifles, carbines, and revolvers."

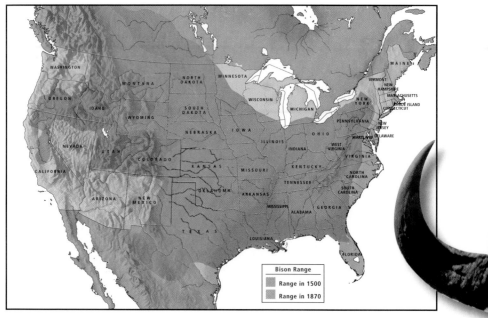

By the 1840s, the buffalo were being killed at increasingly high rates.

Unheard Warnings

Not all Americans approved of the buffalo hunts. The famous naturalist John James Audubon spoke out in 1843. ". . . Before many years the Buffalo, like the Great Auk, will have disappeared," he said. "Surely this should not be permitted?" But most Americans didn't believe that the buffalo would become extinct. Buffalo roamed in herds of millions, after all. No one believed hunting them could ever make a difference.

In 1872, Dr. Brewster Higley wrote a famous poem, "Home on the Range." The first verse is "Oh, give me a home, Where the buffalo roam, And the deer and the antelope play." Have you heard the folk song that the poem became? Sadly, by the time Americans were singing the song, a roaming buffalo was hard to find.

By the end of the 1870s, **bleached** buffalo skeletons covered the Great Plains instead of thundering herds. By the 1890s, Audubon's **suspicions** were coming true. The great wild herds of buffalo weren't endless like everyone had thought. In fact, they were nearly gone.

Between 1872 and 1874, American hunters killed close to four million buffalo.

The End of a Way of Life

The killing of buffalo herds destroyed Native American communities. The Plains Indians needed their sacred buffalo to survive. Indian leaders watched their people die of **starvation** without buffalo meat. One Lakota who lived in the Dakotas explained, "Wherever the whites are established, the buffalo is gone." Those days when life was easy for Native Americans were now gone. Life for the Plains Indians and the buffalo would never be the same.

The loss of the buffalo herds changed the lives of Plains Indians forever.

The Birth of a Movement

Concerns over disappearing wildlife and wilderness grew into America's conservation movement. The settlers who blanketed the young nation throughout the 1800s had changed the land. They pulled down the trees, plowed up prairies, and built farms and towns. North America was losing its natural habitats and the wildlife that depended on them.

Conservationist John Muir was important in establishing Yosemite National Park.

What Is CONSERVATION?

Conservation is an effort to protect wildlife, plants, land, and other natural resources from destruction during transformation. The growing number of human beings has greatly changed our planet. Cities, farms, and roads have replaced much of the world's wilderness, where wildlife once thrived. Conservationists work to save wildlife and wilderness.

Early conservationists believed that the buffalo mattered to North America. They set out to convince Americans that the buffalo was worth saving. Conservationist writer Ernest Baynes gave lectures and showed people buffalo robes and artifacts. He helped turn the buffalo into a symbol of the American frontier.

From Hunter to Crusader

William T. Hornaday was another important early conservationist who helped save the buffalo. Hornaday was a taxidermist. He preserved the bodies of dead animals for display in places such as museums. As Hornaday went about his work, he became worried. He could see that there were fewer and fewer buffalo. Hornaday knew that the American buffalo was headed for extinction.

Milestones in Early Conservation

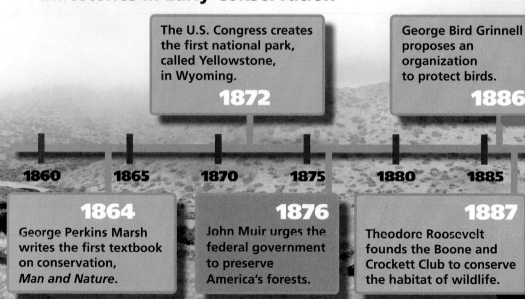

The U.S. Congress creates the first national park, called Yellowstone, in Wyoming.
1872

George Bird Grinnell proposes an organization to protect birds.
1886

1860   1865   1870   1875   1880   1885

1864
George Perkins Marsh writes the first textbook on conservation, *Man and Nature*.

1876
John Muir urges the federal government to preserve America's forests.

1887
Theodore Roosevelt founds the Boone and Crockett Club to conserve the habitat of wildlife.

Hornaday's book *The Extermination of the American Bison* sounded a warning in 1889. The beloved symbol of America, the buffalo, was in danger of disappearing forever. The report called on national and local governments to take action to protect the buffalo. As director of the Bronx Zoological Park, he set up a reserve for buffalo. William Hornaday also helped save the Alaskan fur seal and his work led to the passage of important conservation laws.

The U.S. government creates the first national forest reserve in the area around Yellowstone National Park.

1891

William T. Hornaday raises $100,000 to establish the Permanent Wild Life Protection Fund.

1915

1890   1895   1900   1905   1910   1915

1903

President Theodore Roosevelt begins the National Wildlife Refuge System.

Buffalo Wranglers and Ranchers

Some conservationists worked to change the minds of Americans and lawmakers. Others cared for the few buffalo left and tried to grow their herds. A Native American man named Samuel Walking Coyote saved several orphaned buffalo during the 1870s by taking them to an Indian reservation.

Ranchers created their own buffalo herds, too. Michel Pablo was a Montana rancher who had worked as a "buffalo runner" when he was a young man, helping trap and hunt the great beasts. But later in life he regretted his part in the buffalo's disappearance and began buying buffalo to breed. Hundreds of these buffalo later started herds in Canada.

Rancher C.J. "Buffalo" Jones tried to domesticate the buffalo. He even trained several pairs of buffalo to pull his wagon, instead of horses.

In 1872, the U.S. Congress created the country's first national park, Yellowstone. Within twenty years, Congress had established three more national parks, Yosemite, Sequoia, and Kings Canyon. By the early 1900s, large land areas had been set aside for wild animals. Conservationists had a powerful friend in the 26th U.S. President who served from 1901-1909. Theodore Roosevelt was a naturalist. He understood that our nation's land and wildlife were precious resources and worked to protect them.

Theodore Roosevelt said, "Wild beasts and birds are by right not the property merely of people today but the property of the unborn generations, whose belongings we have no right to squander [waste]."

Hunters often illegally killed buffalo in the early days of Yellowstone National Park.

Buffalo Get Congressional Help

Yellowstone National Park has long been an important home for American buffalo. Hunting isn't allowed in national parks. But during Yellowstone's first years, many hunters broke that rule. In the early 1890s Yellowstone officials were shocked when they counted their buffalo. There were fewer than two dozen! The U.S. Congress took action. In 1894, they passed a law forbidding anyone from hunting or harming wildlife in Yellowstone.

The American Bison Society

The new law helped the buffalo at Yellowstone. But Hornaday and other conservationists wanted to put more buffalo herds on wildlife reserves and in parks. To help win support, Hornaday founded the American Bison Society in 1905.

Their efforts soon began to pay off. In 1907 the U.S. Congress voted to create the first national buffalo preserve. The 8,000-acre Wichita Mountains refuge in Oklahoma soon became home to fifteen buffalo.

You can still see buffalo at the country's first national buffalo preserve. Today it's called the Wichita Mountains Wildlife Refuge.

Year	Number of Buffalo Estimated in the United States
Prior to the 1500s	30 to 70 million
1883	About 1,000
1889	About 550
1929	About 3,385
1934	About 4,000
1950	About 9,252
1970	About 17,000
2005	About 270,000

The National Bison Range is in Montana, where 40 buffalo moved onto their new 18,000-acre home in 1909. Today 350 to 500 buffalo roam there.

Back from the Brink

By the 1930s, Hornaday and the other conservationists had achieved their goal. The American buffalo was saved from extinction. The buffalo thrived in their parks and protected reserves. By 1934, there were 4,000 buffalo living in the United States. Three times that number lived in Canada.

Over the next few decades, conservationists and park rangers managed the buffalo in their care. Part of that job was figuring out how many animals could live comfortably within a certain area.

This ranch is a lot like a cattle ranch. But instead
of beef cattle, ranchers raise buffalo to sell for meat.

Park officials at Yellowstone kept their buffalo
population at around 400 for many decades. Park
rangers gave the buffalo hay, made sure they had
water, and kept predators away. But in 1967 they
decided to turn the herd over to nature. Rangers
stopped managing the buffalo in Yellowstone. There
are more than 3,000 buffalo in Yellowstone today.

Many different groups have worked to make
sure that buffalo never face extinction again.
The National Wildlife Federation keeps track of
the buffalo in Yellowstone, and tries to add more
buffalo to other national parks and reserves.

A buffalo stops traffic in Yellowstone.

A Modern Buffalo Problem in Yellowstone

Buffalo are no longer in danger of extinction, but they still have some problems. Like all animals, buffalo can suffer from diseases and **parasites.** Years ago, scientists discovered that some of the buffalo in Yellowstone were infected with a disease. The disease doesn'thurt the buffalo, but people worry that they'llspread it to cattle. Yellowstone's buffalo sometimes move outside the park while searching for food.

Scientists have found no case of the buffalo giving cows their disease. But cattle ranchers worry that it could happen and have been given the right to kill any buffalo that leaves Yellowstone. Thousands of buffalo have been killed over the years because of this rule. Then, in 1996, ranchers killed 1,000 buffalo outside the park. This was one quarter of the total herd living in Yellowstone!

Conservationists around the world raised their voices in protest. Many groups, such as the Humane Society of the United States, are now demanding that the legal buffalo killing stop. They point out that there is no proof that cattle get the disease from buffalo and that many of the buffalo killed aren't even infected.

Yellowstone's buffalo are wild animals that roam where they please. During the long winters, the buffalo often wander outside the park in search of food.

Conservation groups are working with lawmakers to get the Yellowstone Buffalo Preservation Act passed into law.

The Yellowstone Buffalo Preservation Act

Eventually, lawmakers took up the buffalo's battle again. In 2003 several members of the U.S. Congress introduced a bill. The Yellowstone Buffalo Preservation Act would allow wild buffalo to safely visit nearby lands outside of Yellowstone National Park. If the act is voted into law, it would outlaw the harassment, capture, or killing of any buffalo unless a person is in danger.

Conservationists say there are other ways to deal with buffalo that wander outside Yellowstone. They argue that there's no reason to kill these magnificent symbols of America's wilderness. One suggestion is to move the buffalo that leave Yellowstone to tribal lands. Many Native American communities are interested in having buffalo herds on their reservations. They'd welcome the sacred buffalo back to the land they once shared.

Today, people from all over the world visit the buffalo at Yellowstone and other national parks and reserves across the country. Visitors often see a herd of buffalo thundering across the prairie, or catch them rolling in the dust or mud. Whether you call them buffalo or bison, the buffalo are an amazing sight.

Thanks to the work of early conservationists, you can go buffalo-watching today.

Glossary

bleached *adj.* lightened in color; white

carcasses *n.* dead bodies of animals

decay *n.* the process of rotting

parasite *n.* any living thing that lives on or in another, from which it gets its food, often harming the other in the process

scrawny *adj.* having little flesh; lean; thin; skinny

starvation *n.* dying from lack of food

suspicions *n.* beliefs; feelings; thoughts

tundra *n.* a vast, level, treeless plain in the arctic regions